D06110 59

Created and published by Knock Knock
1635-B Electric Avenue
Venice, CA 90291
knockknockstuff.com

© 2016 Knock Knock LLC
All rights reserved
Knock Knock is a registered trademark of Knock Knock LLC
100 Reasons to Panic is a registered trademark of
Knock Knock LLC
Made in China

Illustrations by Gemma Correll

No part of this product may be used or reproduced in any manner whatsoever without prior written permission from the publisher, except in the case of brief quotations embodied in critical articles and reviews. For information, address Knock Knock.

Where specific company, product, and brand names are cited, copyright and trademarks associated with these names are property of their respective owners.

This book is a work of editorial nonfiction meant solely for entertainment purposes. It is not intended to create actual panic or serve as psychological advice or counsel. In no event will Knock Knock be liable to any reader for any damages, including direct, indirect, incidental, special, consequential, or punitive damages, arising out of or in connection with the use of the information contained in this book. So there.

Every reasonable attempt has been made to identify owners of copyright. Errors or omissions will be corrected in subsequent editions.

ISBN: 978-160106887-3
UPC: 825703-50099-8

10 9 8 7 6 5 4 3

100 Reasons to Panic® about Following Your Dreams

KNOCK KNOCK®
VENICE, CALIFORNIA

1.

People will say you'd have a better chance finding a unicorn.*

*Those are probably the people who told everyone the Tooth Fairy wasn't real.

2.

You'll go broke.*

*Or you'll get rich. Filthy rich!

3.

You have no idea what you're getting yourself into.*

*Isn't that part of the appeal?

4.

Leaving your comfort zone is uncomfortable.*

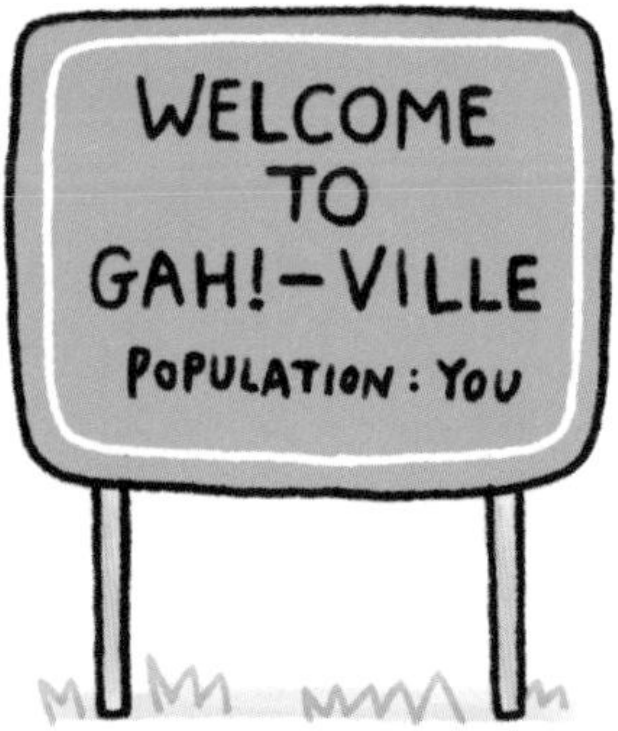

*As long as you don't go into the danger zone, you'll survive.

5.

Anything that can go wrong will go wrong.*

*Think of it as fodder for your future memoir!

6.

You're too shy to network.*

*Being shy just makes you more approachable.

7.

What will other people think?*

*Who cares?

Sayonara, Saturdays and Sundays!*

*Seven days a week devoted to dream-following is way better than a dreary five.

You've got a fear of success.*

*Better that than a fear of failure.

10.

You've got a fear of failure.*

*Join the club.

11.

Friends will grow weary of being your cheerleader.*

*You'll be able return the favor someday.

12.

It's going to be hard.*

*Well, if it doesn't kill you, it will make you stronger-ish.

13.

If you quit your job, you'll lose security, stability, and a regular paycheck.*

*You'll also lose that annoying coworker who keeps swiping your stapler.

14.

People will think you're wasting your time.*

*You're taking the road less traveled.

15.

You'll have to do things that aren't your forte.*

*You're expanding your skill set.

16.

There aren't enough hours in the day to make it all happen.*

*You'll figure out how to survive on coffee and to-do lists.

17.

Plunging into the great unknown is scary.*

*It's your very own choose-your-own-adventure novel!

18.

The odds aren't in your favor.*

*Lotteries aren't either—
but people win 'em all the time.

19.

Following your dreams will make your résumé look weird.*

*Or make it stand out
(just in case you need one again).

20.

You're not sure if it's the right time.*

*If you wait for the "right" time, you'll be waiting a looooong time.

21.

Some people seem to think you need a "real job."*

*That's what they say to make themselves feel better about the daily grind.

22.

Taking risks is, well, risky.*

*So is leaving the house.

23.

Your friends will secretly doubt you.*

*You'll make new friends who don't!

24.

People will laugh at you.*

*You'll grow a thick skin, like a crocodile.

25.

You'll be going against the status quo.*

*You'll be challenging the status quo.

26.

You don't know what the heck you're doing.*

*You'll fall down. You'll get back up.

27.

You'll have to say no to dinner parties and other fun stuff.*

*No more stress about choosing an appropriately priced wine.

vino

28.

You'll have to start from scratch.*

*Everybody has to start somewhere.

29.

More opportunities = more work.*

*More opportunities = more success.

BILL
INVOI
ICE

30.

Paperwork, taxes, legal crap? Yikes.*

*You'll get to refer to your accountant and your lawyer, which will make you sound fancy.

31.

You'll get around to your dream... someday.*

*The sooner you start, the sooner you can ignore all those other things on your to-do list.

32.

People will make assumptions about you.*

*You'll prove them wrong (or right).

33.

with all the stress, you'll forget to eat.*

*Your grocery bills will plummet.

34.

No one "gets" your dream.*

*You're cultivating an air of mystery.

35.

Your brain won't stop.*

*You'll be on the edge of your seat waiting for inspiration to strike. Exciting!

36.

Your stick-to-itiveness is a little intimidating.*

*Better to be feared than to be fearful.

37.

You'll come off as cocky.*

*Or you can wear your confidence like a very cool motorcycle jacket.

38.

Everyone will want your advice for following their dreams.*

*You can bill yourself as a life coach.

39.

What if your dreams are too big?*

*Setting smaller goals will be easy.

40.

What if your dreams are too small?*

*You'll get great practice at setting bigger goals.

EVERYTHING
MUST GO!
SALE
PRACTICALLY
FREE!

41.

No one will want to buy your handmade dream catchers, candles, or mood rings.*

*You might be ahead of the curve on the next Pet Rock.

42.

You'll go into debt.*

*Most companies start out operating in the red.

43.

People will get tired of hearing about your project.*

*You'll be refining your elevator pitch.

44.

You'll be tempted to give up.*

*It'll make the payoff
that much sweeter when you don't.

45.

You feel like you're jumping off a cliff.*

*You'll grow wings! Or invest in a parachute . . .

46.

You'll get new wrinkles.*

*They add character.

47.

You'll have to hire help.*

*You'll have a small (but growing!) empire to rule.

48.

You don't have a mentor.*

*You can be someone else's and create a legacy. Whoa.

49.

Someone will steal your good ideas.*

*What's that saying about imitation and flattery?

50.

You'll have to delegate.*

*You'll get to delegate.

51.

You have so many good ideas, it's hard to focus on just one.*

*If one doesn't work out, at least you have a plan B (or C, or D, or E).

52.

You'll start networking with anyone—or anything—who'll listen.*

*Who knows who—or what—you'll strike up a conversation with.

53.

Things might not go your way.*

*Or they'll be even more awesome than you dreamed.

54.

Sleepless nights will become the new normal.*

*So will power naps!

55.

You'll always be overbooked.*

*You can start charging for your appearances.

56.

No one else believes in your dream.*

*You're a visionary—
you've gotta believe in you first.

57.

Everyone else's life just seems so much more fun.*

*It probably is. (For now, anyway.)

58.

You'll have to do everything.*

*It'll make you understand every part of what you're doing better.

59.

Suddenly, you've developed a nervous twitch.*

*You're quirky!

60.

You'll lose perspective.*

*You'll gain insight.

61.

You'll need to spend a lot of time figuring a lot of stuff out.*

*It'll be like lifting weights—for your brain.

62.

You can't quit your day job yet.*

*Limited hours will force you to be more efficient.

63.

You'll be plagued with self-doubt.*

*It'll add to your charm.

64.

You'll be forced to borrow money from annoying family members.*

*Hey, if they're willing to make you an interest-free loan, maybe they aren't so annoying.

65.

You'll have to ask friends for lots of favors, then end up alienating them.*

*You'll have plenty of peace and quiet.

66.

You're too young.*

*The early bird gets the worm.

67.

You're too old.*

*Better late than never.

68.

Your focus will make you a real bore at cocktail parties.*

*Or fellow partygoers will marvel at your drive and determination.

69.

You'll lose track of time.*

*Better that than watching the clock.

70.

You'll have to say "no" to a lot of stuff.*

*It'll make saying "yes" matter even more.

71.

Trusting your gut makes you a little uneasy.*

*You won't have to rely on psychics, tarot card readers, or fortune cookies.

72.

You've got so many dreams you'll need multiple lifetimes to follow them all.*

*If something doesn't come to fruition, onto the next!

73.

People will think you're nuts.*

*You'll be able to say "Told you so" when you're a huge success.

74.

You're still waiting for fame and fortune.*

*At least there aren't pesky paparazzi capturing you in sweats and sunglasses–yet!

75.

Some people will think it's time you throw in the towel.*

*Haters gonna hate.

76.

Your dream might change.*

*It's called growth and evolution.

77.

You'll have to burn the midnight oil.*

*You'll be nocturnal—just like honey badgers!

78.

You'll stop exercising and eating right.*

*And start wearing elastic-waist pants while eating cookies. Sounds pretty freeing, actually.

PIZZA
ICE
FAMILY SIZE

79.

You'll miss out on major life events.*

*You'll be the freewheeling friend.

80.

Your days will be packed to the gills.*

*Wouldn't you rather be busy than bored?

81.

Turns out your dream is expensive.*

*You'll figure out how to get creative on your taxes.

82.

You'll disappoint your parents.*

*Or make them weep with pride.

83.

You'll neglect your kid(s) and/or pet(s).*

*You're cultivating their independence.

The BIG
BOOK
OF
Bedtime
Stories

84.

You won't have time for a relationship.*

*The last slice of pizza will always be yours.

85.

You'll neglect your relationship.*

*Your partner's golf game will get really good.

86.

You'll start spouting inspirational, self-helpy sayings.*

*You'll be everyone's go-to when they need a pep talk.

87.

You'll become certifiably obsessed.*

*Obsession is just another way to say all-consuming passion.

88.

You'll get weird.*

*You're not weird, you're creative.

89.

You'll get bossy.*

*You're not bossy, you're empowered.

90.

You'll need to start meditating just to cope.*

*You can get a side gig as a spiritual guru. People pay big bucks for that.

91.

Your drive and passion could scare off potential dates.*

*Who needs dates? You've got drive and passion.

92.

You'll get way too into making a vision board.*

You'll have a real work of art to hang above your sofa.

DREAM
$1000
$100
Dream
CAR
inspire
FOCUS
FORBES 500
Luxury
PENTHOUSE
PET TIGERS

93.

You gotta be you—even if that means letting your freak flag fly.*

*If you don't, who else will?

94.

You feel out of touch with regular people sometimes.*

*Regular people are overrated.

95.

You'll kill your plants.*

*You're not wasting water.

96.

You might hit a creative wall.*

*Or you'll break through it, like a superhero.

97.

You'll get in over your head.*

*You'll get to figure out
if you're a sinker or a swimmer.

98.

The struggle is real.*

*So is the potential payoff.

99.

What if you're just not that good?*

*You may as well discover that now, rather than later.

100.

What if you fail?*

*What if you don't?

Don't worry.
It's worth it.